THE CREATOR'S TOY CHEST

THE LIFE OF JESUS

Brett Blair • Illustrated by James Koenig

THIS BOOK BELONGS TO:

_____

How to use this coloring book...

Inside this coloring book, you will find coloring pages and activities with scripture to match each picture. We encourage you to read the corresponding verses to learn more about the life of Jesus. Help your children understand how deep, how wide, and how great His love is for us.

AN ANGEL VISITS MARY WITH A MESSAGE THAT SHE WILL GIVE BIRTH TO A SON AND SHOULD NAME HIM JESUS. FINISH THE PUZZLE BELOW, USING WORDS FROM THE GOSPEL LESSON.

Use the number of letters in each word to match the number of available spaces in the puzzle, making sure each word fits the letters already filled in and that it matches the connecting words.

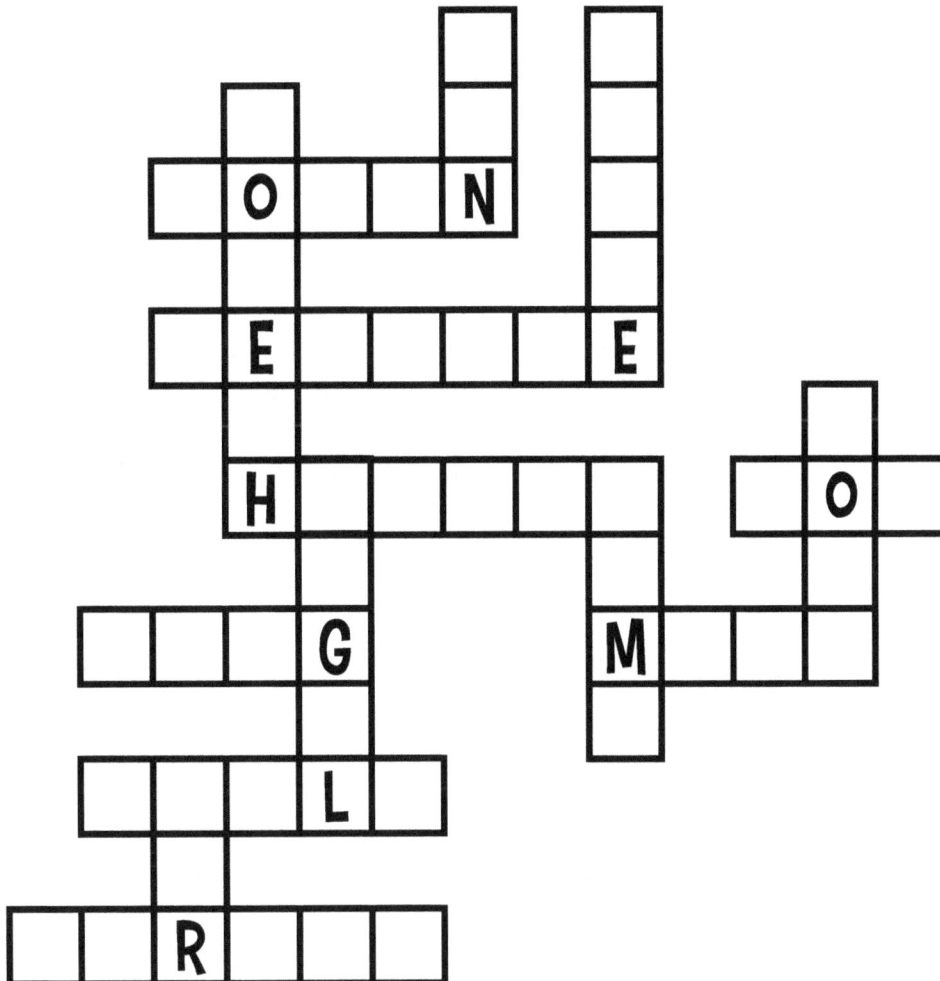

3 LETTER WORDS	4 LETTER WORDS	5 LETTER WORDS	6 LETTER WORDS	7 LETTER WORDS
YOU	NAME	CHILD	JOSEPH	MESSAGE
MAN	HOLY	ANGEL	HAPPEN	
HER	MARY	PEACE	VIRGIN	
	KING	WOMAN		

IN THE GOSPEL STORY PICTURE BELOW ARE HIDDEN OBJECTS.
CAN YOU FIND THEM?

Look for these objects in the big picture.

WHAT NAME IS MARY TO GIVE HER SON?

Color every shape that has a ◆

WHO DOES GOD SEND TO DELIVER THIS MESSAGE TO MARY?

Unscramble each word below and then use the
circled words to uncover the answer to the question above.

1. GNIDKOM

2. LEANG

3. IBHTR

4. NERTANGP

5. LIHCD

6. ZNARAHTE

7. LAREVIET

___ ___ ___ ___ ___ ___ ___

Form words using the letters in this table. Letters must touch and each
letter can only be used once per word. Each word can snake around the box
going up, down, left, right, and diagonal. See how many words you can make.

O	A	N	S
E	E	M	T
L	A	R	K
O	I	L	C

_____   _____   _____

_____   _____   _____

_____   _____   _____

_____   _____   _____

_____   _____   _____

ELIZABETH SAYS MARY AND THE CHILD SHE WILL BEAR ARE... WHAT?

Match and write the letter that fits each piece of the puzzle.

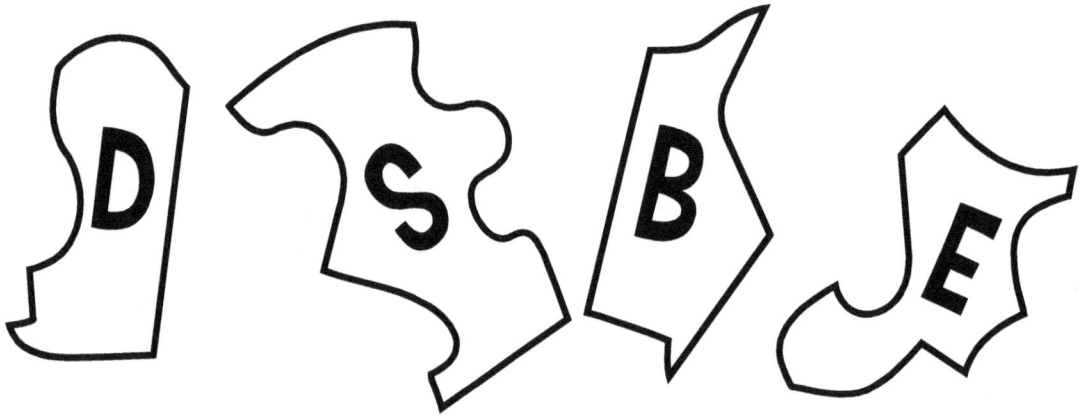

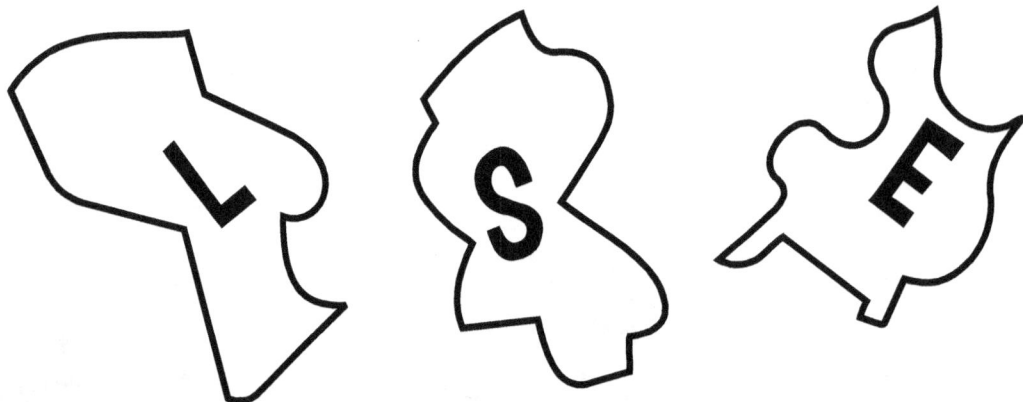

D S B E

L S E

MARY PRAISES GOD WITH A SONG.

Use the code to fill in the missing letters.

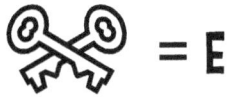

⚓ = A 🗝 = E 𝕴𝕳𝕾 = I 🌈 = O

"G __ D H __ S D __ N __
   🌈   ⚓   🌈   🗝

GR __ __ T TH __ NGS
    🗝 ⚓   𝕴𝕳𝕾

F __ R M __ . H __ LY
  🌈   🗝   🌈

__ S H __ S N __ M __ ."
𝕴𝕳𝕾   𝕴𝕳𝕾   ⚓   🗝

ELIZABETH'S BABY LEAPS IN HER WOMB WHEN SHE HEARS MARY SPEAK. ELIZABETH IS FILLED WITH THE HOLY SPIRIT.

Connect the dots in order (1, 2, 3, 4...).

MARY AND JOSEPH TAKE JESUS TO THE TEMPLE IN JERUSALEM TO PRESENT HIM TO THE LORD. IN THE PUZZLE BELOW ARE WORDS FROM THE GOSPEL LESSON. SEE IF YOU CAN FIND THEM!

Circle the words found in the Word List below.
They can be across, up, down or diagonal (both forward and backward).

WORD LIST:

CEREMONY	JERUSALEM	CHILD
TEMPLE	PROMISE	MESSIAH
PIGEONS	PROPHET	BLESSING
SIMEON	SACRIFICE	SWORD
DEDICATE	ANNA	CHOSEN

```
E  U  C  W  I  Y  N  E  Z  Y  Y  C
C  P  J  H  X  L  L  D  H  N  H  H
I  I  T  E  O  P  K  J  O  A  A  I
F  G  C  S  M  S  P  M  M  N  I  L
I  E  B  E  M  R  E  B  C  N  S  D
R  O  T  L  O  R  L  N  I  A  S  H
C  N  E  M  E  L  A  S  U  R  E  J
A  S  I  C  F  S  K  H  X  B  M  W
S  S  D  R  O  W  S  I  M  E  O  N
E  G  G  O  D  E  D  I  C  A  T  E
T  E  H  P  O  R  P  Z  N  D  Y  T
U  V  V  M  S  U  E  E  U  G  Q  O
```

WHEN HE SEES MARY AND JOSEPH ENTER THE TEMPLE, HE TAKES JESUS IN HIS ARMS AND GIVES THANKS TO GOD. WHO IS HE?

Write the name for each picture.
Then place the letters from each box on the lines below.

☐ _ _ _

_ _ ☐ _ _

_ _ _ ☐ _

_ _ ☐ _

_ ☐ _ _ _

_ _ _ ☐ _

_ _ _ _ _ _

WHEN JOSEPH AND MARY FINISH AT THE TEMPLE, THEY RETURN TO THEIR HOMETOWN OF NAZARETH IN GALILEE.

Draw a path for Mary, Joseph and Jesus from the Temple back to Galilee

WHEN THEY SEE THE STAR, THE MAGI ARE OVERJOYED. WHAT HAPPENS WHEN THEY SEE THE CHILD JESUS?

Write the words from the stars on the lines below.

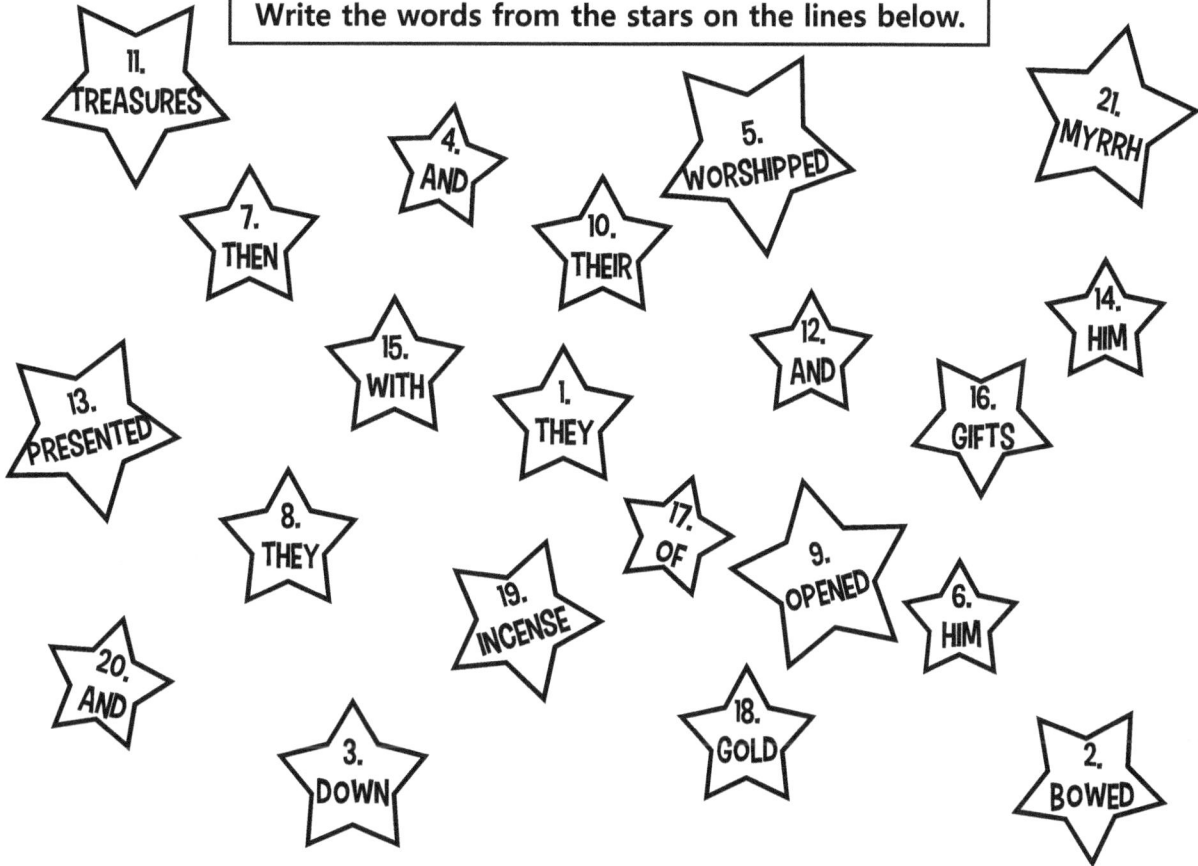

11. TREASURES

4. AND

5. WORSHIPPED

21. MYRRH

7. THEN

10. THEIR

14. HIM

15. WITH

1. THEY

12. AND

16. GIFTS

13. PRESENTED

8. THEY

17. OF

9. OPENED

6. HIM

19. INCENSE

20. AND

18. GOLD

3. DOWN

2. BOWED

_____ _____ _____ _____
1   2   3   4

_____ _____ . _____ ____
5   6   7   8

_____ _____ _____ _____
9   10   11   12

_____ _____ _____ _____ _____
13   14   15   16   17

_____ , _____ , _____ _____ .
18   19   20   21

[Answer: They bowed down and worshiped him. Then they opened their treasures and presented him with gifts of gold, incense and myrrh.]

WHEN THE WISE MEN SEE THE BABY, THEY WORSHIP HIM.
THEY ALSO GIVE HIM SPECIAL GIFTS.

Circle the two images that are exactly alike.

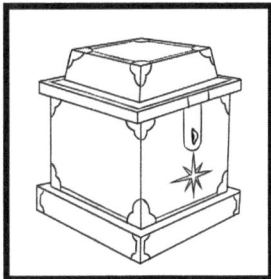

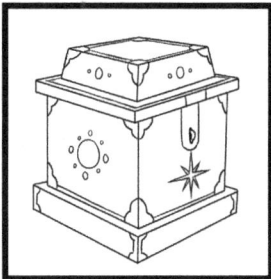

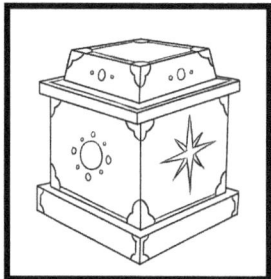

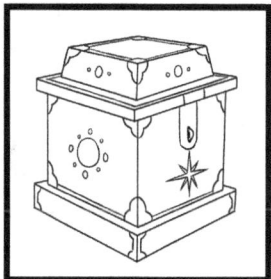

WITH A FRIEND, TAKE TURNS DRAWING
AN X AND O IN THE TIC TAC TOE GAMES BELOW.
TRY TO GET 3 IN A ROW TO WIN THE GAME.

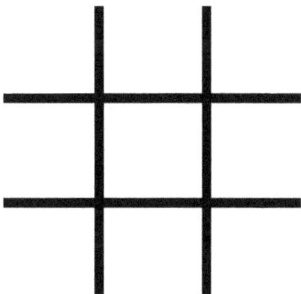

WHEN JESUS TURNS TWELVE, HE GOES TO JERUSALEM WITH HIS PARENTS. ON THE WAY BACK HOME, NO ONE CAN FIND JESUS, SO MARY AND JOSEPH GO BACK TO JERUSALEM TO LOOK FOR HIM.

Help them find Jesus.

AFTER SEARCHING FOR 3 DAYS, THEY FIND JESUS IN THE TEMPLE.

WHAT DOES JESUS SAY WHEN HE FINDS OUT THEY ARE LOOKING FOR HIM?

Shade in every box that contains these letters: C G J P Q Z
Write the remaining letters in order in the blanks below.

C	D	J	G	C	I	J	P	Z	C	G	D
J	P	C	G	N	Q	Z	G	T	J	J	P
Y	O	Z	J	P	J	U	C	G	Q	K	N
G	C	O	Q	Z	W	Z	I	J	P	G	C
P	J	G	Z	H	C	J	P	A	G	C	Q
D	G	T	C	J	P	G	Z	C	Q	O	G
J	Q	P	G	C	B	E	J	G	Z	Q	P
C	G	I	J	P	G	Z	C	Q	N	P	J
P	M	Y	Z	Q	C	F	P	J	G	C	C
Z	J	G	C	A	P	Q	T	G	J	J	H
G	C	E	P	J	G	R	Z	C	Q	S	G
H	Q	Q	G	C	Z	C	G	O	U	P	J
C	G	J	S	P	P	G	E	C	G	Z	Q

" __ __ __ __ __ ' __ __   __ __ __ __   __ __ __ __

__   __ __ __   __ __   __ __

__ __   __ __ __   __ __ __ __ __ __ ' __

__ __ __ __ ?"

JESUS WENT HOME WITH HIS PARENTS, WHERE HE GROWS IN WISDOM AND STATURE, AND IN FAVOR WITH GOD AND PEOPLE.

Find and circle 10 differences between these two pictures.

IN THIS GOSPEL LESSON, JESUS IS BAPTIZED
BY JOHN IN THE JORDAN RIVER.

HOW MANY NEW WORDS CAN YOU MAKE
USING THE LETTERS IN THE WORD "BAPTIZED"?

Write your new words in the spaces provided below.

BAPTIZED

_____ _____ _____

_____ _____ _____

_____ _____ _____

_____ _____ _____

_____ _____ _____

_____ _____ _____

_____ _____ _____

WITH A FRIEND, TAKE TURNS CONNECTING LINES BETWEEN THE DOTS
TO FORM SQUARES. WHEN YOUR LINE MAKES A SQUARE, YOU WIN THAT
SQUARE. WRITE YOUR INITIALS IN IT AND THEN TAKE ANOTHER TURN.
THE ONE WITH THE MOST SQUARES WINS THE GAME!

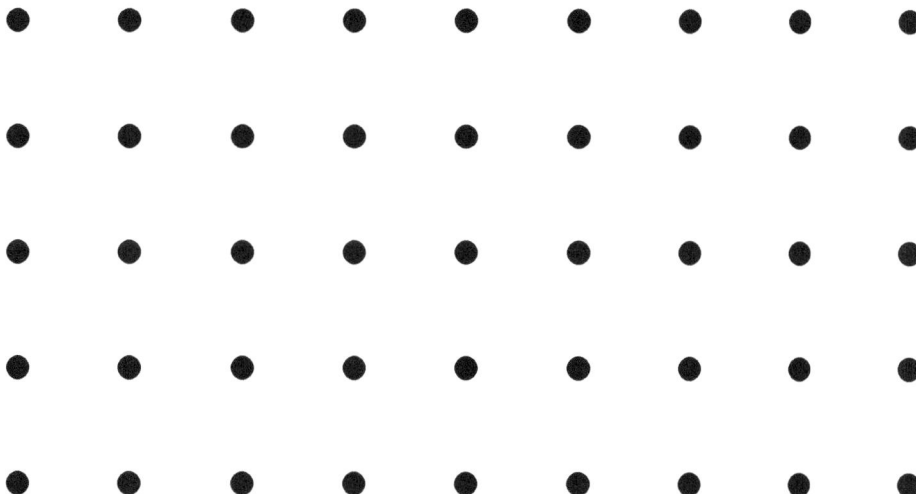

•   •   •   •   •   •   •   •   •

•   •   •   •   •   •   •   •   •

•   •   •   •   •   •   •   •   •

•   •   •   •   •   •   •   •   •

•   •   •   •   •   •   •   •   •

WHEN JESUS COMES OUT OF THE WATER, HE SEES THE HEAVENS OPEN AND THE SPIRIT COMING DOWN ON HIM LIKE A DOVE.

Find and circle 10 differences between these two pictures.

AFTER JESUS IS BAPTIZED, A VOICE COMES FROM HEAVEN.
WHAT DOES THIS VOICE (GOD) SAY?

Use the code to find out

A = 1 I = 5 O = 9 T = 13 Y = 17 D = 2 L = 6

P = 10 U = 14 E = 3 M = 7 R = 11 V = 15

H = 4 N = 8 S = 12 W = 16

"___ ___ ___   ___ ___ ___   ___ ___
9+8 6+3 10+4   2-1 7+4 6-3   5+2 11+6

___ ___ ___,   ___ ___ ___ ___   ___
8+4 7+2 12-4   8+8 3+1 10-1 14-7   3+2

___ ___ ___ ___;   ___ ___ ___ ___   ___ ___ ___
3+3 5+4 12+3 7-4   13+3 12-7 15-2 2+2   15+2 18-9 20-6

___   ___ ___   ___ ___ ___ ___
4+1   2-1 6+1   17-1 8-5 4+2 3+3

___ ___ ___ ___ ___ ___ ___."
5+5 8-2 10-7 1+0 6+6 4-1 1+1

IN THESE SCRIPTURES, JESUS IS BAPTIZED BY JOHN AND TEMPTED BY SATAN.

Fill in this Crossword Puzzle using clues from these two Gospel lessons from Mark 1.

ACROSS

2. A voice from heaven said,
"You are my Son, whom I _____." (v. 11)
5. Jesus said we need to "repent and
_____ the good news." (v. 15)
7. How many days did Jesus spend in
the wilderness? (v. 13)
8. Who came and helped Jesus while
he was in the wilderness? (v. 13)
10. Who baptized Jesus? (v. 9)

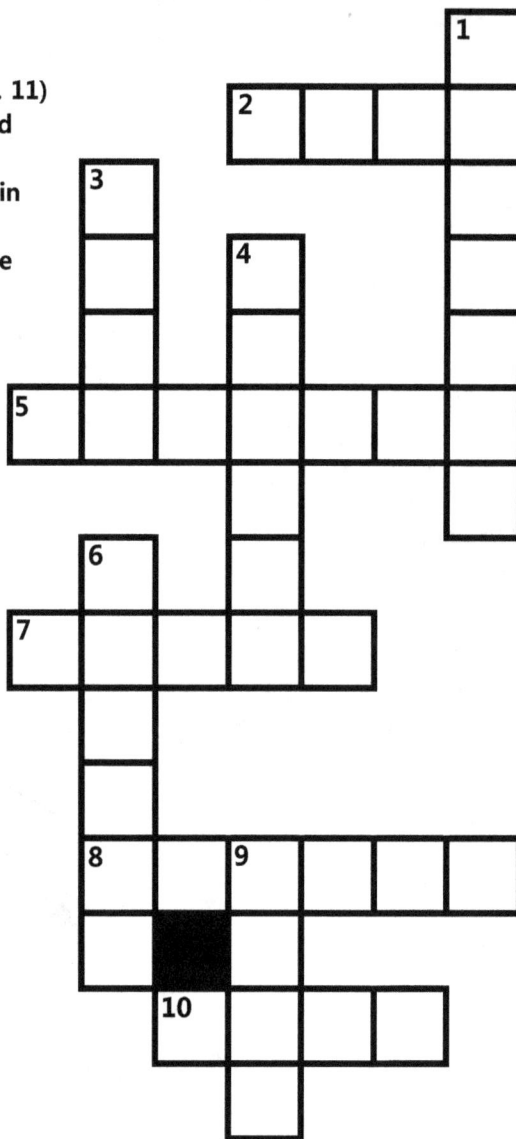

DOWN

1. Jesus was _____ by Satan in the wilderness (v. 13)
3. The Spirit came down on Jesus like what kind of bird? (v. 10)
4. Who sent Jesus out into the wilderness? (v. 12)
6. Jesus was baptized in the _____ River. (v. 9)
9. Jesus went into Galilee, preaching the _____ news of God. (v. 14)

[Answers: 1. TEMPTED 2. LOVE 3. DOVE 4. SPIRIT 5. BELIEVE 6. JORDAN 7. FORTY 8. ANGELS 9. GOOD 10. JOHN]

JESUS GOES INTO GALILEE PROCLAIMING THE GOOD NEWS OF GOD. THERE ARE SOME HIDDEN OBJECTS IN THIS PICTURE BELOW. CAN YOU FIND THEM?

Look for these objects in the big picture.

JESUS SAYS, "I WILL SEND YOU OUT TO FISH FOR PEOPLE."

Color every shape that has a ♥

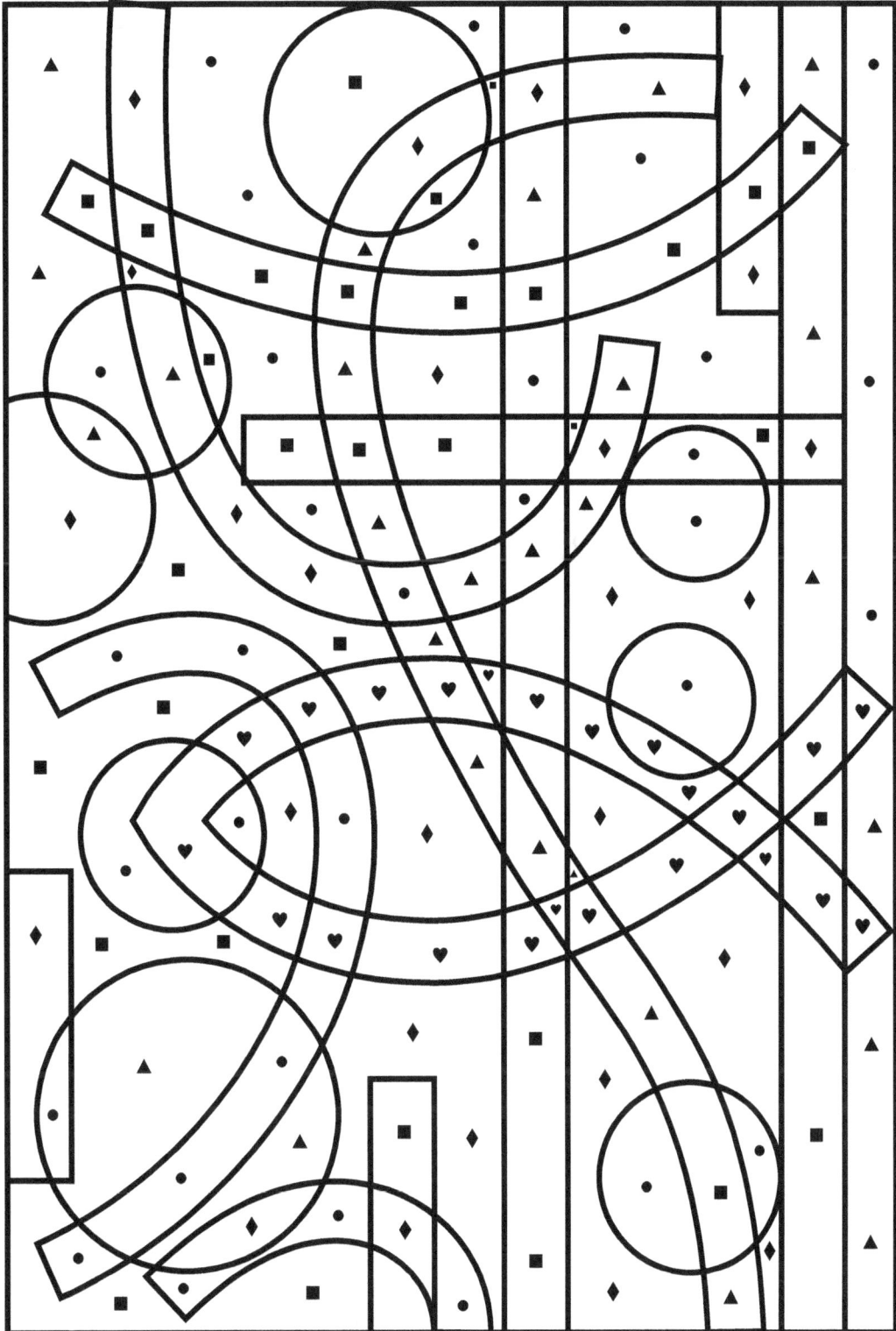

JESUS IS WALKING BESIDE THE SEA OF GALILEE AND SEES SIMON AND ANDREW CASTING THEIR NET INTO THE LAKE TO CATCH FISH. WHAT DOES JESUS SAY TO THEM?

Connect the dots and unscramble the words along the way.
Write them in order on the lines below.

4. EM

3.

5.

2. LOFLOW

6. NAD

10.

2.

8.

7.

1. MOCE

9.

29.

11. LILW

27. 28.

13.

26. EPLOPE

25.

14. NSDE

24. ROF

18.

17. UTO

23.

12.

19.

15. OYU

16.

21.

22. SFHI

20. OT

" ___ ___ ___ ___ , ___ ___ ___ ___ ___ ___ ___ ___ ___ ___ ,

___ ___ ___ ___ I ___ ___ ___ ___ ___ ___

___ ___ ___ ___ ___ ___ ___ ___ ___

___ ___ ___ ___ ___ ___ ___ ___ ___ ___ . "

TWO SETS OF BROTHERS, SIMON AND ANDREW & AND JAMES AND JOHN, LEAVE THEIR NETS WHEN JESUS INVITES THEM TO FOLLOW HIM.

Use the number of letters in each word to match the number of available spaces in the puzzle, making sure each word fits the letters already filled in and that it matches the connecting words.

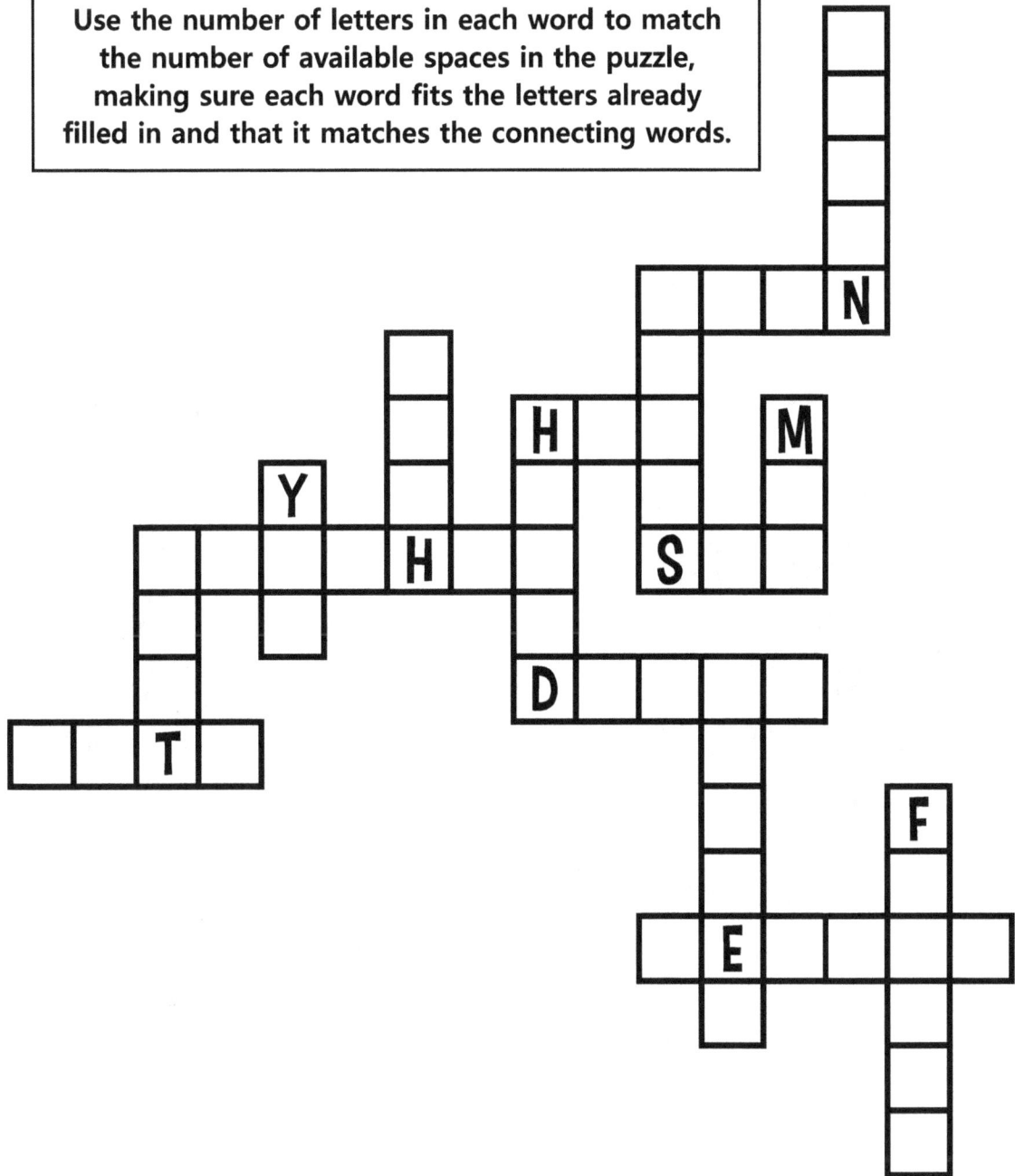

3 LETTER WORDS	4 LETTER WORDS	5 LETTER WORDS	6 LETTER WORDS	7 LETTER WORDS
YOU	FISH	SIMON	FOLLOW	BROTHER
HIM	BOAT	DELAY	ANDREW	
MEN	NETS	HIRED	PEOPLE	
SON	JOHN	JAMES		

PHILIP LEAVES TO FIND NATHANIEL AND TELL HIM ABOUT JESUS.

Help Philip find his friend.

JESUS TELLS NATHANIEL HE WILL SEE GREATER THINGS TO COME. WHAT ELSE DOES JESUS SAY?

Use this letter maze to find the sentence below.
Move only in straight lines: up, down, left and right.

"Very truly I tell you, you will see heaven open, and the angels of God ascending and descending on the Son of Man."

START

V	T	R	R	U	J	R	V	M	R	I	X	C
E	R	Y	T	L	E	Y	S	E	T	I	R	I
L	E	T	I	Y	Q	L	Y	S	F	A	C	E
L	Y	O	A	P	A	E	J	D	D	Z	T	I
C	O	U	Y	O	U	W	Y	N	E	I	L	R
O	D	H	N	G	R	I	R	A	S	U	D	E
V	A	E	T	D	I	L	P	G	C	C	J	G
E	S	H	E	E	S	L	Q	N	E	I	T	P
N	E	N	Z	A	D	M	E	I	N	J	Y	X
O	R	V	S	O	F	N	N	D	D	H	E	S
P	T	E	L	I	G	O	E	D	I	T	N	O
E	M	J	E	R	G	D	C	P	N	N	O	N
N	D	H	G	S	D	A	S	K	G	O	F	O
A	G	V	N	G	J	Y	V	E	A	X	M	R
N	I	I	A	D	G	M	J	L	R	O	A	D
D	T	H	E	D	G	M	J	L	R	O	N	D

FINISH

JESUS IS SLEEPING IN THE BOAT WHEN A STORM APPEARS.
THE DISCIPLES ARE AFRAID AND WAKE JESUS UP.

Connect the dots in order (1, 2, 3, 4...).

AFRAID, THE DISCIPLES ASK JESUS, "TEACHER, DON'T YOU CARE IF WE DROWN?" WHAT DOES JESUS SAY TO CALM THE WIND AND WAVES?

Follow the arrows to find the correct letter for each puzzle.
For example, M ➡➡⬇ = R
Find M in the box below. From there move two letters to the right, and one letter down. Your answer is R.

" __ __ __ __ __!   __ __   __ __ __ __ __!"
  1 2 3 4 5   6 7   8 9 10 11 12

---

1. V ⬅⬆⬆ = ___

2. X ➡➡⬇ = ___

3. O ⬅⬆⬆ = ___

4. W ➡⬇⬅⬅ = ___

5. R ⬅⬅⬅ = ___

6. M ⬅⬆⬆⬆ = ___

7. C ➡⬇➡⬇ = ___

8. G ⬇⬇⬅⬅ = ___

9. Z ⬅⬅⬆ = ___

A	B	H	I	D	B
T	F	J	W	Q	I
U	K	E	C	O	G
X	L	M	B	I	V
Y	T	U	S	R	E
E	N	Q	Z	U	P

10. D ⬇⬇⬇ = ___

11. J ⬇⬇⬅ = ___

12. A ⬇➡⬇⬇ = ___

THE DISCIPLES ARE TERRIFIED BY WHAT THEY SEE. WHAT DO THEY SAY?

Write the letter that is missing in each box on the lines above.

"___ ___ ___   ___ ___   ___ ___ ___ ___?"

| V X Y Z | F G I J | L M N P | | G H J K | Q R T U | | R S U V | G I J K | F G H J | R T U V |

(WHO IS THIS)

___ ___ ___ ___   ___ ___ ___   ___ ___ ___ ___

| C D F G | T U W X | B C D F | L M O P | | Q R S U | E F G I | C D F G | | T U V X | F G H J | K L M O | A B C E |

(EVEN THE WIND)

A ___ ___   ___ ___ ___   A ___   ___ ___ ___

| M O P Q | C E F G | | R S U V | G I J K | B C D F | | U V X Y | | S T U W | D F G H | P Q R T |

(AND THE WAVES)

___ ___ ___ ___   ___ ___ ___."

| N P Q R | A C D E | D F G H | V W X Z | | F G I J | H J K L | L N O P |

(OBEY HIM)

LARGE CROWDS FOLLOW JESUS. JESUS ASKS HIS DISCIPLES
WHERE THEY CAN GET ENOUGH FOOD TO FEED ALL THE PEOPLE.

THEY FIND A BOY WITH FIVE LOAVES AND TWO FISH.

Circle the picture below that matches what the boy gives Jesus.

JESUS TAKES THE FOOD, GIVES THANKS TO GOD, AND THEN SHARES IT WITH THE WHOLE CROWD. WHEN EVERYONE HAS HAD ENOUGH TO EAT, WHAT DOES JESUS AND THE DISCIPLES SAY AND DO NEXT?

Match the missing halves to complete the puzzle.

_____ING	PIE_____	_____VE
BAS_____	_____TED	EAT_____
BAR_____	LOA_____	FI_____
_____ERED	GA_____	_____CES

"JESUS SAID, " _____THER THE _____CES THAT ARE

LEFT OVER. LET NOTH_____ BE WAS_____."

SO THEY GATH_____ THEM AND _____LLED

TWEL_____ _____KETS WITH THE PIE_____ OF THE

FIVE _____LEY _____VES LEFT OVER BY THOSE

WHO HAD _____EN."

JESUS FEEDS FIVE THOUSAND PEOPLE WITH 5 LOAVES AND 2 FISH.
THE DISCIPLES THEN FILL 12 BASKETS WITH LEFTOVER BREAD.

Circle the two images that are exactly alike.

WITH A FRIEND, TAKE TURNS DRAWING
AN X AND O IN THE TIC TAC TOE GAMES BELOW.
TRY TO GET 3 IN A ROW TO WIN THE GAME.

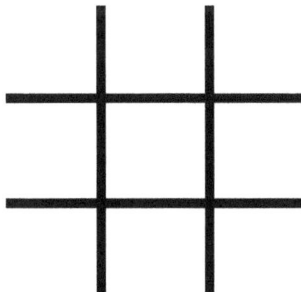

JESUS IS THE GOOD SHEPHERD. HE LAYS DOWN HIS LIFE FOR THE SHEEP.

Connect the dots in order (1, 2, 3, 4...).

WHAT DOES JESUS SAY ABOUT HIS OTHER SHEEP?

Follow the instructions to change each given word into a new word.
Write the new words in order on the numbered blanks below.

1. CAVE .... CHANGE C TO H

2. SHEER .... CHANGE R TO P

3. THAN .... CHANGE N TO T

4. LOT .... CHANGE L TO N

5. TEN .... CHANGE T TO P

6. MIST .... CHANGE I TO U

7. BLING .... CHANGE L TO R

8. PILL .... CHANGE P TO W

9. CHOICE .... CHANGE CH TO V

10. WHERE .... CHANGE W TO T

11. FLICK .... CHANGE I TO O

"I _____ other _____ _____ are _____ of
    1   2   3   4

this sheep _____. I _____ _____ them also. They
           5   6   7

too _____ listen to my _____ , and _____ shall
    8   9   10

be one _____ and one shepherd."
         11

JESUS WANTS TO BRING ALL THE SHEEP INTO THE SAME PEN, SO THAT THERE IS ONE FLOCK AND ONE SHEPHERD.

Help Jesus get the sheep into the same sheep pen.

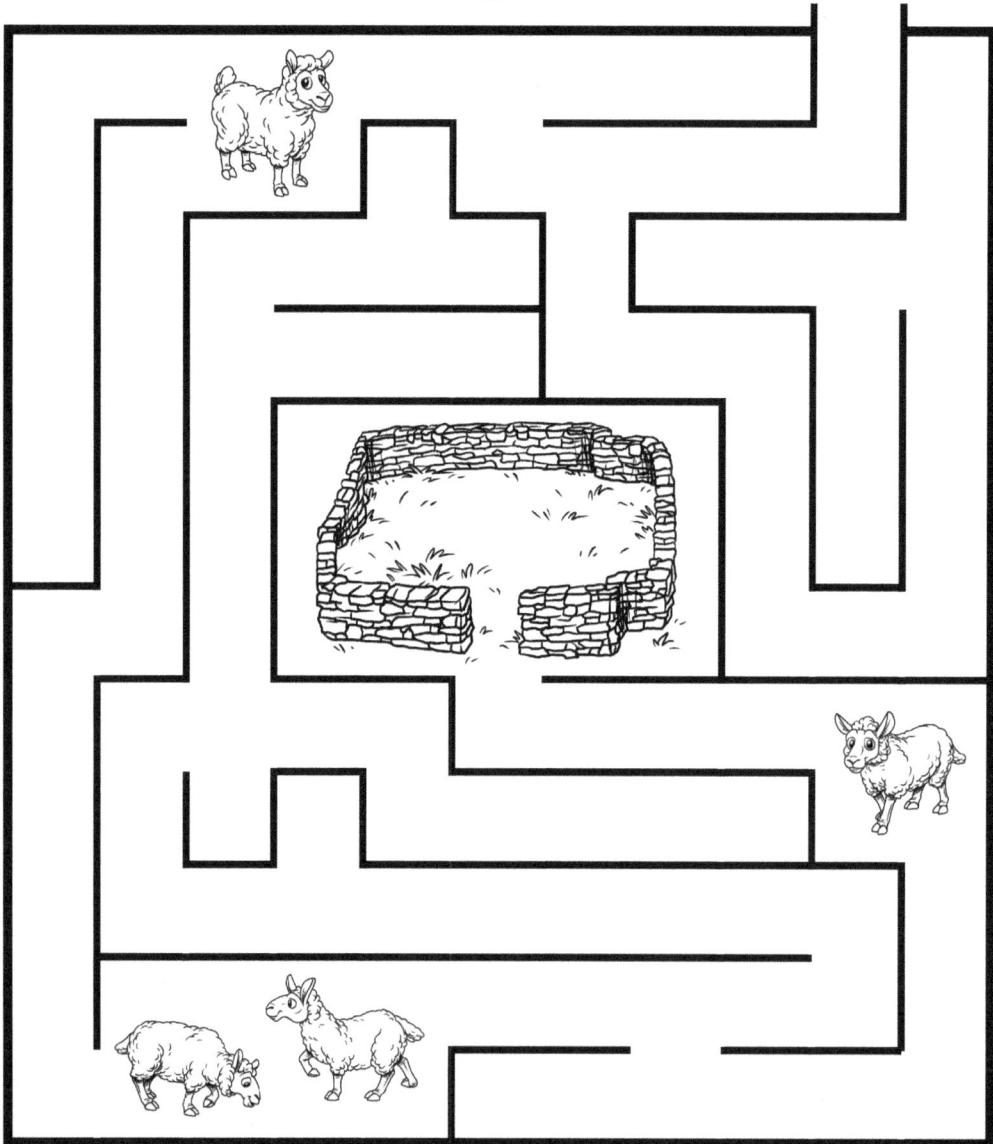

PEOPLE BRING THEIR CHILDREN TO JESUS
SO HE CAN PLACE HIS HANDS ON THEM.

Help the little children get to Jesus.

THE DISCIPLES WANT TO SEND THE PARENTS AND THEIR CHILDREN AWAY. WHAT DOES JESUS SAY WHEN HE SEES THEM DOING THIS?

Use this code to reveal what Jesus said:

A	B	C	D	E	F	G	H	I	J	K	L	M	N	O	P	Q	R	S	T	U	V	W	X	Y	Z
Z	Y	X	W	V	U	T	S	R	Q	P	O	N	M	L	K	J	I	H	G	F	E	D	C	B	A

"___ ___ ___   ___ ___ ___   ___ ___ ___ ___ ___
O   V   G   G   S   V   O   R   G   G   O   V

___ ___ ___ ___ ___ ___ ___   ___ ___ ___ ___   ___ ___
X   S   R   O   W   I   V   M   X   L   N   V   G   L

___ ___'   ___ ___ ___   ___ ___   ___ ___ ___
N   V   Z   M   W   W   L   M   L   G

___ ___ ___ ___ ___ ___   ___ ___ ___ ___'   ___ ___ ___
S   R   M   W   V   I   G   S   V   N   U   L   I

___ ___ ___   ___ ___ ___ ___ ___ ___ ___   ___ ___
G   S   V   P   R   M   T   W   L   N   L   U

___ ___ ___   ___ ___ ___ ___ ___ ___   ___ ___
T   L   W   Y   V   O   L   M   T   H   G   L

___ ___ ___ ___   ___ ___   ___ ___ ___ ___ ___."
H   F   X   S   Z   H   G   S   V   H   V

WHAT DOES JESUS DO AFTER HE TAKES THE CHILDREN IN HIS ARMS?

> Write the name for each picture.
> Then place the letters from each box on the lines below.

 1. ☐ __ __

 2. __ ☐ __ __ __

 3. __ __ __ __ ☐

 4. __ ☐ __ __

 5. __ __ ☐ __

 6. __ __ ☐ __

 7. ☐ __ __ __

He __ __ __ __ __ __ __ them.
   1   2   3   4   5   6   7

JESUS IS UPSET WITH THE PEOPLE DOING THE SELLING. WHAT DOES HE SAY?

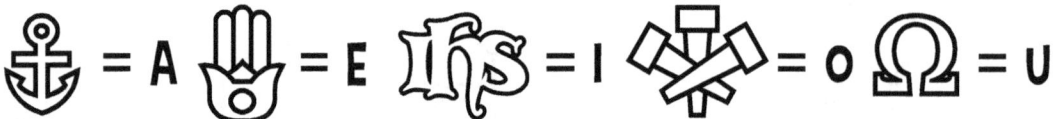

Use the code to fill in the missing letters.

⚓ = A 🖐 = E 𝕴𝕳𝕾 = I ✳ = O Ω = U

"ST __ P T __ RN __ NG
 Ω 𝕴𝕳𝕾

MY F __ TH __ R'S
⚓ 🖐

H __ __ S __ __ NT __
 Ω 🖐 𝕴𝕳𝕾

__ M __ RK __ T."
⚓ ⚓ 🖐

JESUS IS MAD THAT PEOPLE ARE SELLING THINGS IN THE TEMPLE.

Circle the 3 things below that people were selling.

WITH A FRIEND, TAKE TURNS DRAWING
AN X AND O IN THE TIC TAC TOE GAMES BELOW.
TRY TO GET 3 IN A ROW TO WIN THE GAME.

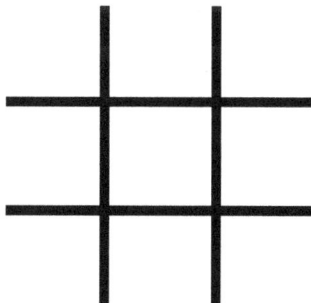

JESUS SITS ON THE DONKEY AND RIDES IT INTO JERUSALEM.
IN THE PICTURE BELOW ARE HIDDEN OBJECTS. CAN YOU FIND THEM?

Look for these objects in the big picture.

THE PEOPLE WAVE PALM BRANCHES AND
SHOUT PRAISES AS JESUS RIDES INTO THE CITY.

Connect the dots in order (1, 2, 3, 4...).

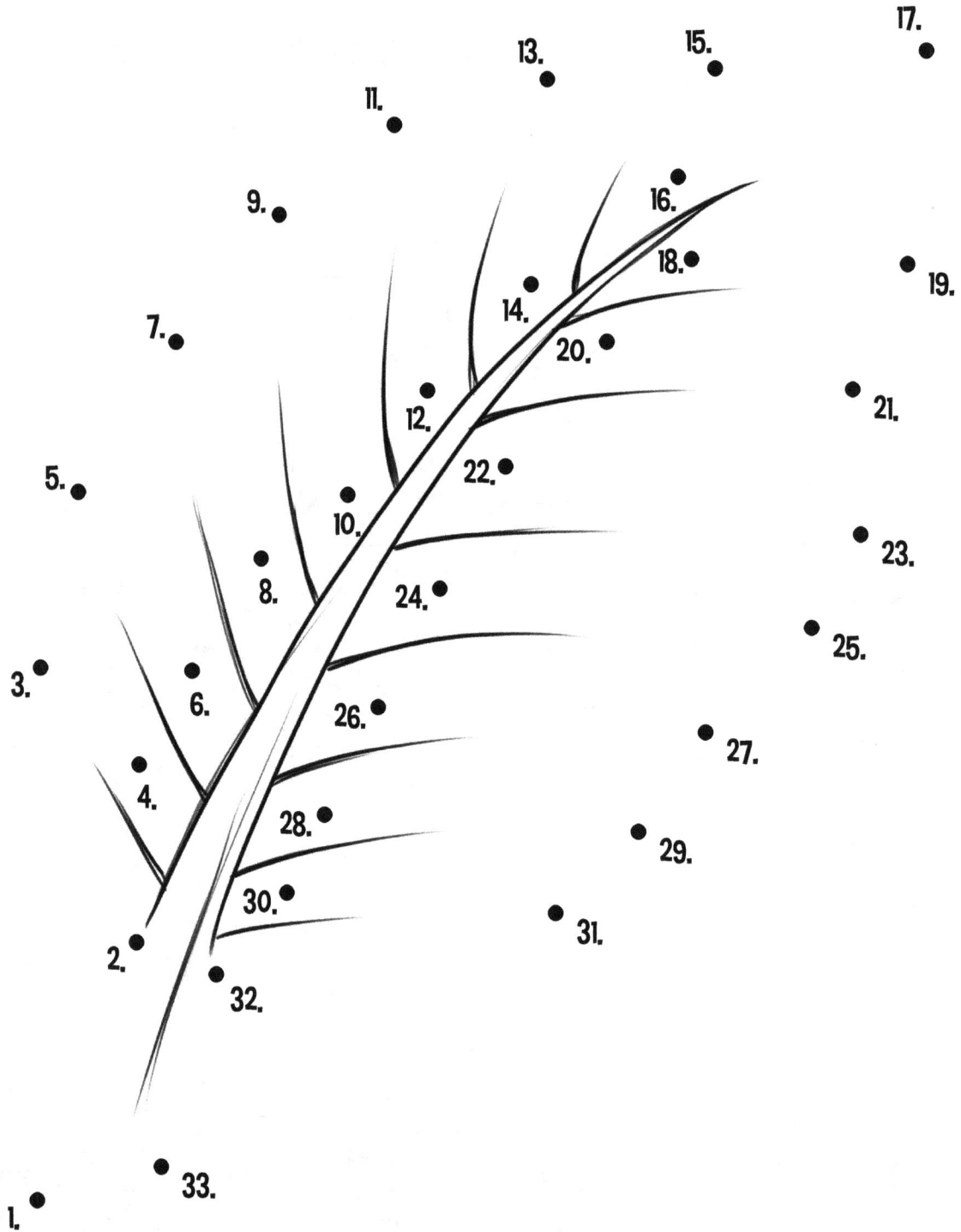

17.

13.

15.

11.

9.

16.

18.

7.

14.

19.

20.

12.

21.

5.

22.

10.

23.

8.

24.

25.

3.

6.

26.

27.

4.

28.

29.

30.

31.

2.

32.

33.

1.

WHAT DOES THE CROWD SHOUT AS JESUS ENTERS THE CITY?

Unscramble each world below and then use the circled words to uncover the answer to the question above.

1. HOSUT ___ (○) ___ ___ ___

2. WOLOLF ___ ___ ___ (○) ___

3. SICDIPLE ___ ___ (○) ___ ___ ___ ___

4. KCLAO ___ ___ ___ (○) ___

5. ESBHCRAN ___ ___ ___ (○) ___ ___ ___ ___

6. DYEONK ___ ___ (○) ___ ___ ___

7. VEHANE ___ ___ (○) ___ ___ ___

"___ ___ ___ ___ ___ ___!"

Form words using the letters in this table. Letters must touch and each letter can only be used once per word. Each word can snake around the box going up, down, left, right, and diagonal. See how many words you can make.

_____ _____ _____

_____ _____ _____

_____ _____ _____

_____ _____ _____

_____

B	E	A	D
M	Y	T	I
C	M	S	E
W	E	Z	A

Possible Words:
beat, item, sea, beat, tease, sew, bet, tie,
sit, bets, yet, set, bye, cyst, daisy, met,
zesty, ease, tad, west, meaty, tea, easy,
stay, meat, day, stem, diet, die, ate

[Answers: 1. SHOUT 2. FOLLOW 3. DISIPLE 4. CLOAK
5. BRANCHES 6. DONKEY 7. HEAVEN..."HOSANNA IS ANSWER TO FINAL Q]

WHAT DOES JESUS ASK GOD TO DO FOR HIS DISCIPLES?

Fill in the blanks by finding where the first and second symbol intersect on the graph code.

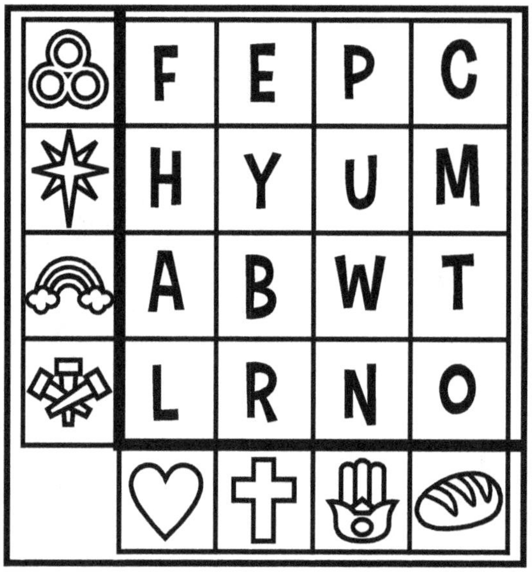

F E P C
H Y U M
A B W T
L R N O

[Answer: "Holy Father, protect them by the power of your name."]

JESUS ASKS GOD TO GIVE HIS DISCIPLES JOY.

Circle the faces below that look full of joy.

JESUS PRAYS FOR HIS DISCIPLES.
IN THE PUZZLE BELOW ARE WORDS FROM THE GOSPEL READING.
SEE IF YOU CAN FIND THEM!

Circle the words found in the Word List below.
They can be across, up, down or diagonal (both forward and backward).

WORD LIST:

PRAYER	REVEAL	FULFILL
WORLD	TRUTH	WORD
JESUS	SANCTIFY	OBEY
FATHER	GLORY	BELIEVE
PROTECT	REMAIN	POWER

```
U  K  S  O  A  H  D  I  R  P  P  X  X
B  C  A  R  G  R  D  E  R  V  X  Q  E
D  R  N  Q  O  M  H  O  B  E  Y  R  O
L  E  C  W  T  T  D  V  E  D  E  U
Z  W  T  V  A  E  F  U  K  K  Y  Y  F
M  O  I  F  C  R  E  V  E  A  L  A  F
E  P  F  T  L  L  I  F  L  U  F  R  W
S  V  Y  Q  G  R  L  Y  W  Y  J  P  O
H  O  E  B  X  A  E  Q  R  E  G  M  R
D  W  S  I  Q  I  S  M  S  O  J  J  L
C  T  L  Z  L  E  G  U  A  D  L  N  D
H  T  U  R  T  E  S  T  U  I  V  G  T
K  C  J  X  W  G  B  R  D  H  N  Z  M
```

PILATE CALLS JESUS TO HIM AND ASKS, "ARE YOU THE KING OF THE JEWS?

In the picture below are 6 hidden crowns:

Can you find all 6?

JESUS SAYS, "MY KINGDOM IS NOT OF THIS WORLD. MY KINGDOM IS FROM ANOTHER PLACE."
FINISH THE PUZZLE BELOW, USING WORDS FROM THE GOSPEL LESSON.

Use the number of letters in each word to match the number of available spaces in the puzzle, making sure each word fits the letters already filled in and that it matches the connecting words.

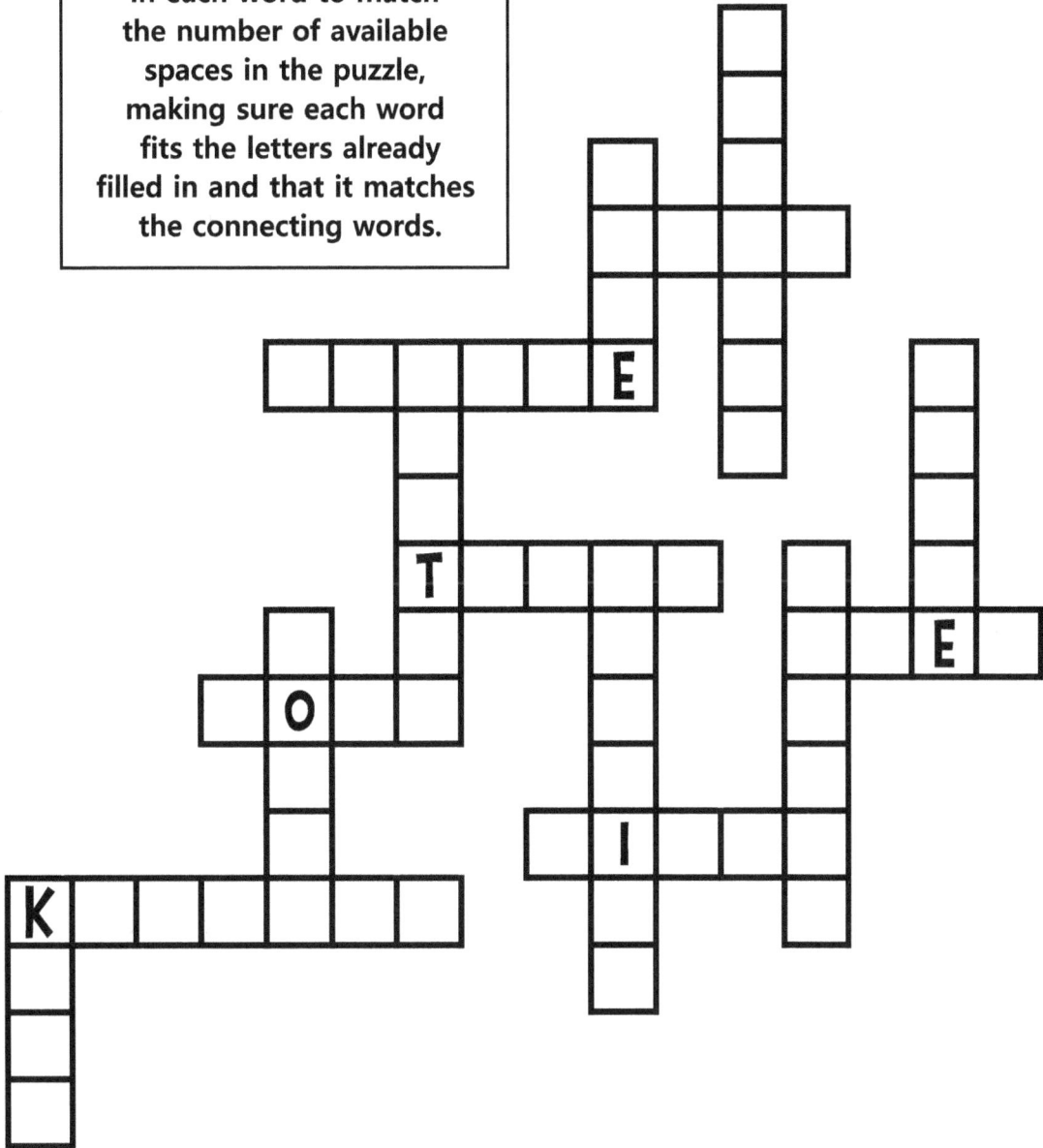

4 LETTER WORDS	5 LETTER WORDS	6 LETTER WORDS	7 LETTER WORDS
KING	TRUTH	PALACE	KINGDOM
IDEA	WORLD	PILATE	TESTIFY
BORN	FIGHT	LISTEN	PRIESTS
DONE	PLACE		
OVER			

WHAT DOES JESUS SAY TO PILATE NEXT?

Solve each math problem below by circling the correct answer.
Then write the word by each answer in the lines below.

①
11+2 =
10 CAUSE
11 TRUTH
12 WAY
13 REASON

②
13-7 =
4 HERE
5 SENT
6 BORN
7 GONE

③
7X2 =
5 WENT
9 COME
14 CAME
15 GO

④
5+4 =
9 WORLD
10 LAND
11 CITY
12 TOWN

⑤
9-3 =
5 SPEAK
6 TESTIFY
7 JUDGE
8 WITNESS

⑥
4X4 =
0 FACTS
4 WORLD
8 PEOPLE
16 TRUTH

⑦
4-2 =
2 EVERYONE
3 ALL
4 PEOPLE
8 WE

⑧
8+7 =
12 LOVE
13 FAVOR
14 BACK
15 SIDE

⑨
2X0=
0 LISTENS
1 HEARS
2 SPEAKS
3 COMES

" The _____ I was _____ and _____
1   2   3

into the _____ is to _____ to the
4   5

_____ . _____ on the _____ of truth
6   7   8

_____ to me ."
9

WHEN MARY SEES THE EMPTY TOMB, SHE RUNS TO TELL THE DISCIPLES.

Help Mary get to Peter and John.

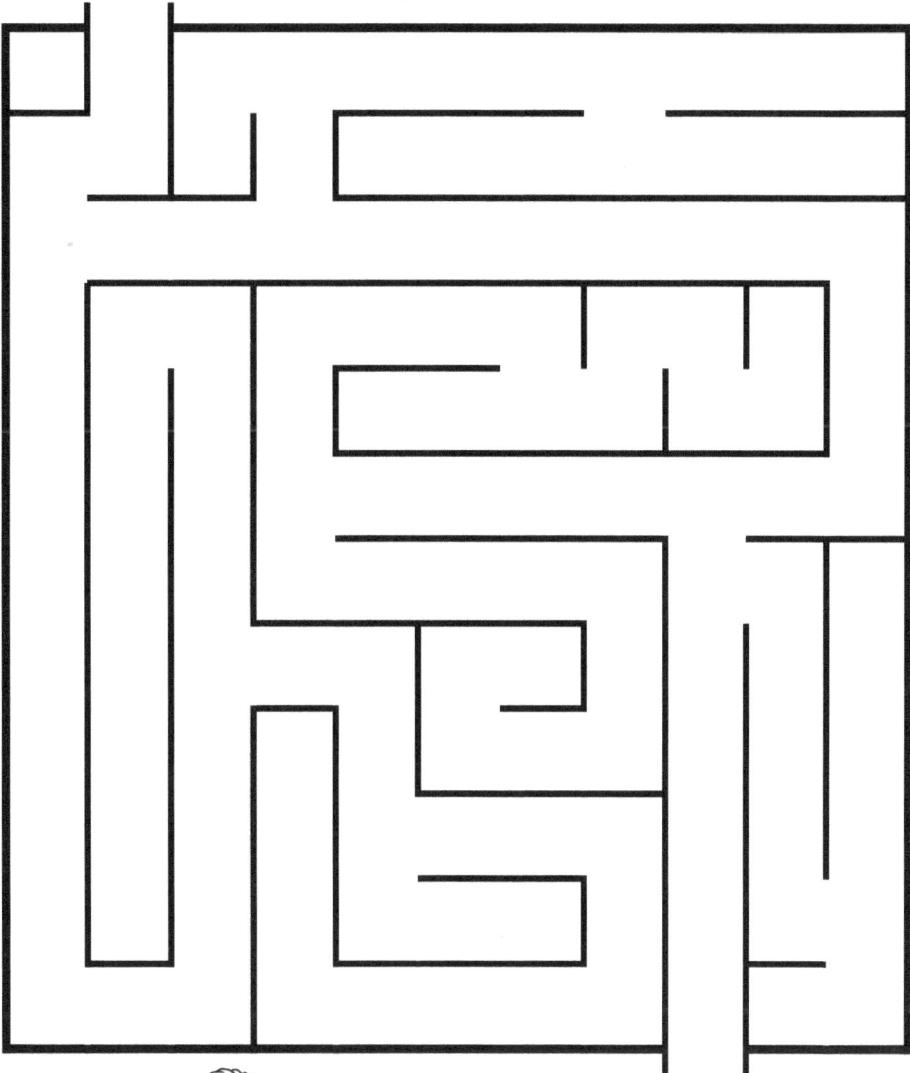

WHAT DOES MARY MAGDALENE SAY TO THE DISCIPLES AFTER HER DISCOVERY?

Use this letter maze to find the sentence below.
Move only in straight lines: up, down, left and right.

"They have taken the Lord out of the tomb, and we don't know where they have put him!"

START

T	H	T	R	U	J	R	V	M	R	I	X	C
E	E	Y	H	L	B	E	S	E	T	E	T	I
L	E	V	A	V	Q	H	E	S	F	H	O	E
L	Y	E	A	P	A	T	L	D	D	T	M	I
C	O	T	A	K	E	N	O	N	E	F	B	A
O	D	H	N	G	R	I	R	U	T	O	D	N
V	A	E	T	D	I	L	D	O	C	C	W	D
E	S	H	Q	E	S	L	Q	N	O	D	E	P
N	E	N	Z	W	D	N	K	T	N	J	D	X
O	R	V	S	W	W	O	N	A	X	H	O	S
P	T	R	E	H	W	O	E	D	I	T	N	O
E	M	J	R	E	E	Y	M	P	N	V	O	N
N	D	H	G	R	H	H	H	K	G	O	F	O
A	G	V	N	E	T	A	V	E	E	X	M	R
N	I	S	A	D	G	H	J	P	U	T	H	W
D	T	H	E	F	Z	M	J	L	R	M	I	Y

FINISH

THE OTHER DISCIPLE, JOHN, JOINS PETER INSIDE THE TOMB.
HE SEES THE EMPTY TOMB AND BELIEVES.

Find and circle 10 differences between these two pictures.

THE DICIPLES WERE TOGETHER, WITH THE DOORS LOCKED OUT OF FEAR. WHEN JESUS SUDDENLY APPEARS BEFORE THEM, WHAT DOES HE SAY?

Follow the arrows to find the correct letter for each puzzle.
For example, S ➡➡⬇ = Y
Find S in the box below. From there move two letters to the right, and one letter down. Your answer is Y.

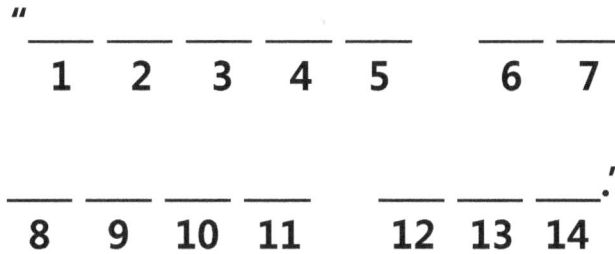

" ___ ___ ___ ___ ___   ___ ___
  1   2   3   4   5   6   7

___ ___ ___ ___   ___ ___ ___."
 8   9   10   11   12   13   14

---

1. J ⬅⬅⬆ = ___

2. T ⬅⬇⬇ = ___

3. I ➡➡⬆⬆ = ___

4. G ⬆⬆ = ___

5. V ➡➡⬆ = ___

6. D ⬇⬇⬅ = ___

7. T ➡⬆⬆⬆ = ___

8. Z ⬇⬅⬅ = ___

9. K ⬅⬇⬇ = ___

10. J ⬇⬇⬅⬅⬆ = ___

W	X	E	Z	C	Q
V	P	X	R	X	A
C	Y	D	J	G	B
S	T	K	A	O	M
O	B	Y	F	H	Z
E	I	U	W	L	C

11. U ⬆➡➡ = ___

12. S ⬇➡➡ = ___

13. T ➡➡➡ = ___

14. G ⬇⬇⬇⬅⬅ = ___

THOMAS IS NOT IN THE ROOM WHEN JESUS APPEARS.
WHAT DOES THOMAS SAY HE NEEDS, TO BELIEVE IT WAS JESUS?

Match Thomas' words to the picture in the other column.

"UNLESS I SEE
THE NAIL MARKS...

...AND PUT MY FINGER
WHERE THE NAILS WERE...

...AND PUT MY HAND
INTO HIS SIDE,
I WILL NOT BELIEVE."

THOMAS SEES JESUS AND BELIEVES. WHAT DOES THOMAS SAY?

Write the 1st letter of each picture in the box above it.

" ☐ ☐   ☐ ☐ ☐ ☐

and

☐ ☐   ☐ ☐ ☐ !"

JESUS IS ALIVE AND LOVES YOU!

AUTHOR OF THE CREATOR'S TOY CHEST SERIES

Brett Blair is a graduate of Yale Divinity School, a minister, publisher, and a writer. Born in Memphis Tennessee he resides in Sarasota Florida with his wife and 3 children.

He is a United Methodist Minister and the founder of Sermons.com which for 20 years has served ministers in the US and abroad with resources for worship and preaching. The Creator's Toy Chest begins a new chapter in reaching a new generation for Christ. At CTC we believe that kids are bright enough to understand the Gospel but critical enough to see when quality work has gone into the resources they use. It's our mission to give them both.

You can view other resources and children's books from The Creator's Toy Chest series at **www.creatorstoychest.com**.

ILLUSTRATOR OF THE CREATOR'S TOY CHEST SERIES

James Koenig is an illustrator who resides in Arizona. He lives with his wife, Corissa, and dog, Bailey.

James started drawing almost as soon as he was born. It was always a passion of his and eventually made it a career when he grew up. Whether or not he has truly grown up is still up for debate. James has illustrated for over 40 books over his career so far. Along with books, he has also developed characters and artwork for countless products, toys, games, and more. You can see more of his work at his website: **www.freelancefridge.com**.

www.ingramcontent.com/pod-product-compliance
Lightning Source LLC
Chambersburg PA
CBHW081220020426
42331CB00012B/3055